THE MISSION OF SPIRITUAL SCIENCE

&

OF ITS BUILDING AT DORNACH SWITZERLAND

(1916)

"This booklet contains a lecture given by me, after a series of objections had been brought forward in a lecture from another quarter against the views summed up under the name "Anthroposophy" or "Spiritual Science." In this booklet, therefore, the true form of spiritual science is delineated in contradistinction to the imaginary one."

Dr. Rudolf Steiner

ISBN 1-56459-705-9

FOREWORD

THIS booklet contains a lecture given by me, after a series of objections had been brought forward in a lecture from another quarter against the views summed up under the name " Anthroposophy " or " Spiritual Science." I came to know of these objections through the circumstance that the lecturer himself had them printed in a newspaper. When the occasion of the observations contained in this booklet is borne in mind, it might seem as if their special publication were unjustified. With regard to this it may be said that even though the objections in question were, to begin with, only the subject of a single lecture, they are the ones with which it is intended from many quarters and in divers repetitions to refute the spiritual science (Anthroposophy) referred to in this booklet. They are to a certain extent typical " refutations." They are typical, not only because of what is alleged, but because of the *manner* in which an attitude is taken towards that to which objections are raised. This manner is characteristic. It is often the case that people do not fix their attention upon

3

what spiritual science says and direct their attack against this, but they fabricate an idea of what they *think* it says, and then attack this idea. A curious position results. The one attacked may quite agree with his opponent in his judgment of all that is attacked, and yet he is obliged to find that he is condemned, together with the distorted idea formed of him. The following example is particularly characteristic for this form of attack. A building is being erected for the purposes of Anthroposophy (Spiritual Science). This is to be a " College of Spiritual Science." In the artistic form of the building it is sought to realise that for which this Spiritual Science can give the stimulus. The building is intended to bring to artistic expression that for which it is the frame, as it were. Certainly, the manner in which this is accomplished may be objected to from one or another artistic point of view. And the author of this pamphlet is far from thinking that what is being attempted in this building will be fully attained. But he is endeavouring to see that every sort of inartistic symbolism or allegorising is kept far removed from it. It is only necessary to open one's eyes in order to find that, when it is viewed, there is absolutely nothing symbolical or allegorical of the kind often met with where is found unhealthy mysticism or such like and not spiritual science such as is to be pursued in this building. Yet in spite of this, one of the objections raised against this building is : " One who enters this building will find all kinds of mysterious symbols which are incomprehensible to the non-initiated, etc., etc." In this way what we wish to attain in the building is successfully attacked, but only through the attack being directed against something which does not exist, and which, if it were really so, the one attacked would repudiate just as his opponent does. But by far the most of what is brought against the spiritual science we represent runs on this line. First a caricature of it is made, which sets all scientific thought at defiance, and then this caricature is attacked with the weapons of science. Another caricature is made, which is attacked from the point of view of religious feeling, whereas in truth no religious confession would have the slightest occasion to think anything but kindly of this spiritual science, if its true form were kept in view instead of a caricature of it.

In such a state of affairs it is almost impossible to do anything more than meet these attacks by stating the actual aims of spiritual science or Anthroposophy, and the lines it takes. I endeavoured to do this in the lecture upon which this pamphlet is based. Above all it is shown that the attacks are inapposite, because they are directed against self-made targets and not against Anthroposophy.

In this pamphlet, therefore, the true form of spiritual science is delineated in contradistinction to the imaginary one.

In the " Afterword," a little more is said which amplifies the hints given in the lecture. The word " we " often occurs in the lecture ; this is because I spoke to a certain extent as the representative of the movement in which Anthroposophy is cultivated.

RUDOLF STEINER

April 1916

IF I try to put forward this evening something about so-called spiritual science, about the way in which it is to be dealt with in the building at Dornach with which you are acquainted, and about that building itself, it is in no wise my intention to propagandise or arouse feeling either for Spiritual Science or for the Building.

I have specially in view the consideration of certain misunderstandings, which are known to exist with reference to the aims of the Anthroposophical Society. I will begin with the way in which a more or less unknown thing is judged when it makes its appearance anywhere. It is very easy to understand that anyone unfamiliar with a subject sees in its name something by means of which he thinks he can understand it. Anthroposophy and the Anthroposophical Society are names which have become more widely known than they formerly were, through the building at Dornach. "Anthroposophy" is by no means a new name. When some years ago there was a question of giving our cause a name, I thought of one which had become dear to me because a Professor of Philosophy, Robert Zimmermann, whose lectures I heard in my youth, called his chief work *Anthroposophy*. This was in the 'eighties of the nineteenth century. Moreover, the name Anthroposophy takes us still farther back into literature. It was already used in the eighteenth century, indeed, still earlier. The name, therefore, is an old one ; we are applying it to something new. For us it does not mean, " Knowledge of human beings." That would be against the express intention of those who gave the name. Our science itself leads us to the conviction that within the physical human being there lives a spiritual, inner one—as it were, a second human being.

Whereas that which man can learn about the universe through his senses and through the intellect which relies upon sense-observation may be called " Anthropology," that which the inner, spiritual human being can know may be called " Anthroposophy."

Anthroposophy is therefore the knowledge of the spiritual human being, or spirit-man, and that knowledge is not confined to man, but is a knowledge of everything which the spirit-man can perceive in the spiritual world, just as physical man observes physical things in the world. Because this second human being, the inner one, is the spiritual human being, the knowledge which he acquires may be called

" Spiritual Science." And this name is even less new than the name Anthroposophy. That is to say, it is not even unusual, and it would be a complete misunderstanding if anyone were to think that I, as has been said, or anyone closely connected with me, had coined the name " Spiritual Science." The name is used everywhere where it is thought possible to attain knowledge which is not merely physical science, but knowledge of something spiritual. Numbers of our contemporaries call history a spiritual science, call sociology, political economy, æsthetics, and the philosophy of religion spiritual sciences. We use the name, only in a somewhat different sense, that is, in the sense that spirit is to us something real and actual, whereas most of those who nowadays speak of history, political economy, etc., as spiritual sciences, resolve the spirit into abstract ideas.

I will now also say something about the development of our Anthroposophical Society, because errors have been circulated on the subject. For instance, it is said that our Anthroposophical Society is only a kind of development out of what is called the " Theosophical Society." Although it is true that what we aim at within our Anthroposophical Society placed itself for a time within the framework of the general Theosophical Society, yet our Anthroposophical Society must on no account be confused with the Theosophical Society. And in order to prevent this, I must bring forward something, apparently personal, about the gradual rise of the Anthroposophical Society.

It was about fifteen years ago that I was invited by a small circle of people to give certain lectures on spiritual science. These lectures were afterwards published under the title, *Mysticism and Modern Thought*. Up till then I had, I may say, endeavoured as a solitary thinker to build up a view of the world which on the one hand fully reckons with the great, momentous achievements of the physical sciences, and on the other hand desires to rise to insight into spiritual worlds.

I must expressly lay stress on the fact that at the time when I was invited to speak to a small circle in Germany on the subject connected with spiritual science already mentioned, I did not depend in any way upon the works of the writer Blavatsky or of Annie Besant, nor did I take them particularly into consideration. These books, in their way of looking at things, were but little in keeping with my view of the world. I had at that time endeavoured, purely out of what I had discovered for myself, to give some points of view about spiritual worlds. The lectures were printed ; some of them were very soon translated into English, and that by a dis-

tinguished member of the Theosophical
Society, which at that time was particularly
flourishing in England ; and from this quarter
I was urged to enter the Theosophical Society.
At no time had I any idea, if the occasion
should have presented itself in the Theosophical Society, of bringing forward anything else but what was built up on the
foundation of my own, independent method of
research.

That which now forms the substance of our
anthroposophical view of the world, as studied
in our circle of members, is not borrowed from
the Theosophical Society, but was represented
by me as something entirely independent, and
represented within that Society in consequence
of an invitation from it, until it was there found
heretical and turned out ; and what had thus
always been an independent part of that
Society was further developed and further
built up in the now wholly independent
Anthroposophical Society.

Thus it is an entirely erroneous conception
to confuse in any way that which is living
within the Anthroposophical Society with what
is represented by Blavatsky and Besant. It is
true that Blavatsky has in her books put
forward important truths concerning spiritual
worlds, but mixed with so much error that
only one who has accurately investigated these
matters can succeed in separating what is

important from what is erroneous. Hence our Anthroposophical movement must claim to be considered wholly independent. This is not put forward from want of modesty, but merely in order to place a fact in its objectively right light.

Then came the time when it became necessary to represent in an artistic, dramatic form that which our spiritual science, our Anthroposophy, gave in its teachings. We began doing this in 1909 at Munich. From that time onward to the year 1913 we tried every year to give artistic expression in dramatic representations at Munich to that which our investigations lead us to acknowledge is living in the world as spiritual forces, as spiritual beings.

These dramatic performances were at first given in an ordinary theatre. But it soon became evident that an ordinary theatre cannot be the right framework for that which, in a certain way, was to enter the spiritual development of humanity as a new thing. And thus the necessity arose for having a building of our own for such representations, and for the prosecution of our spiritual science generally and the art which belongs to it ; a building which, moreover, in its form of architecture is an expression of what it is desired to accomplish. At first it was thought that it would be well to erect such a building in Munich.

When this proved impossible, or, at any rate, extremely difficult, the possibility arose of our erecting the building at Dornach near Bâle, on a very beautiful hill, where a large piece of land was offered us by a Swiss friend, who had this ground at his disposal, and who has our cause at heart. And thus, through easily comprehensible circumstances, it has come about that the building has been erected just in the north-western corner of Switzerland.

And now, before speaking further about the Dornach building, I should like to deal with the mission of spiritual science itself. It may be quite easy to understand that spiritual science or Anthroposophy, in the sense here intended, is misunderstood. One who has become conversant with this spiritual science finds it entirely comprehensible that many misunderstandings should be brought against it; and one who knows the course taken by the spiritual development of mankind, will not be surprised at such misunderstandings. Opinions such as, " It is mere imagination ; it is dreaming," or perhaps worse, are comprehensible. Those things which have entered the spiritual evolution of mankind for the first time have, as a rule, been received in the same way as this spiritual science. Moreover, it may very easily appear as if this spiritual science resembled certain older views of the universe which are

not exactly popular at the present time. I
the objects of spiritual science or Anthropo
sophy are looked at merely from the outside
it may be thought that they resemble those
pursued by the Gnostics in the first Christian
centuries. But one who really learns wha·
our spiritual science is will find that it bears no
more resemblance to the Gnosis than does the
natural science of the present day to the natural
science of the eighth or sixth century A.D.
True, resemblances may be found between all
possible things, if only a sufficient number of
their distinguishing features be eliminated.
It may, for instance, be said, "This spiritual
science, this Anthroposophy, desires to know
the world in a spiritual way. The Gnostics
also desired to know the world in a spiritual
way. Consequently spiritual science and the
Gnosis are one and the same."

In a similar manner may Anthroposophy be
confused, let us say, with alchemy, with the
magic of the Middle Ages. But this is all due
to a complete misapprehension, a complete
misunderstanding of the real aims of this
spiritual science or Anthroposophy. In order
to gain insight into this matter, it is necessary
to look first at the modern method of thought
in natural science, which for three or four
centuries has been developing out of quite a
different method of thought. It is necessary
to realise what it meant for mankind when

three or four centuries ago the revolution took
place which may be expressed in the words :
up to that time everyone, learned and ignorant
alike, believed that the earth stood still in the
midst of the universe, and that the sun and
stars revolved round the earth. It may be
said that in consequence of what Copernicus,
Galileo, and others taught at that time, the
ground under men's feet was made movable.
Now, when the movement of the earth is
looked upon as a matter of course, there is no
feeling left of the surprising effect produced
upon humanity at large by this and everything
connected with it.

Now what natural science then sought to do
for the interpretation and explanation of the
mysteries of nature, spiritual science seeks to
do for the spirit and soul at the present time.
In its fundamental nature, spiritual science
desires to be nothing else than something for
the life of soul and spirit similar to what
natural science then became for the life of
external nature. One who believes, for instance, that our spiritual science has something
to do with the ancient Gnosis quite ignores
the fact that with the view of the world taken
by natural science, something new entered the
mental evolution of mankind, and that as a
result of this new element, spiritual science is
to be something similarly new for the investigation of spiritual worlds.

Now spiritual science, if it is to do the same for spirit that natural science has done for nature must investigate quite differently from the latter. It must find ways and means of penetrating into the sphere of the spiritual, a domain which cannot be perceived with outer physical senses, nor apprehended with the intellect which is limited to the brain.

It is still difficult to speak intelligibly about the ways and means found by spiritual science for penetrating into the spiritual sphere, because the spiritual world is generally considered, from the outset, as something unknown, indeed, as something which must necessarily remain unknown. Now spiritual science shows that the perceptive powers which man has in ordinary life, and which he also uses in ordinary science, are by no means able to penetrate into the spiritual world. In this respect spiritual science is in full accord with certain branches of natural science. Only natural science does not know certain faculties in man, which are latent within him, but capable of being developed.

It is again difficult to speak of these faculties at the present time, for the reason that they are, far and wide, confused with all manner of diseased phenomena in man. For instance, there is much talk nowadays of the possibility of man's acquiring certain abnormal faculties, and the natural scientist thereupon declares that it is true that they may be acquired, but they are only due to the fact that the otherwise normal nervous system and brain have become abnormal and diseased. In every case in which the investigator in natural science is correct in making such a statement, the spiritual investigator at once acknowledges it. But the aim of spiritual science should not be confused with what is often and widely called " clairvoyance," in a superficial way. Neither should spiritual science be confused with that which appears under the name of spiritualism, etc., etc. The essential thing is this, that this spiritual science should be distinguished from everything that is in any way due to diseased human predispositions.

In order to make myself quite intelligible on this point, I must indicate, if only in a few words, the manner in which the spiritual investigator institutes his researches. The method of research in spiritual science is founded on something which has nothing to do with the soul-forces of man in so far as they are bound up with his bodily organism. If, for instance, it is said that spiritual science is founded on what is to be attained through some form of asceticism, or on something for which the nervous system is prepared and stimulated in a certain way, or that it results from the bringing of spirits into manifestation

3

in an outer, physical way—all such assertions would be utterly inaccurate. That which the spiritual investigator has to do to gain the faculty of looking into the spiritual world, consists exclusively of processes of the spirit and soul; they have nothing to do with changes in the body, nor with visions arising from a morbid bodily life.

The spiritual investigator will be most careful not to let the body have any influence over that which he spiritually perceives. I mention by the way that if, for instance, a large number of the adherents of spiritual science are vegetarians, this is a matter of taste, which in principle has nothing to do with spiritual methods of research. It has only to do with a certain manner of making life easier—I would even say, with a more comfortable regulation of life, since it is easier to work in a spiritual way if no meat be eaten.

The main point is that spiritual science, with its methods of research, only begins where modern natural science leaves off. Humanity is indebted to the view of the world taken by natural science for what I would call a logic which educates itself by the facts of nature itself.

An important method of training has come in, among those who have studied natural science, with regard to the inner handling of thought. I will now try to make clear by a comparison the relation of spiritually scientific research to that of natural science. The mode of thought used by the investigator in natural science I would compare with the forms of a statue. The logic developed from the outer facts of nature has something lifeless in it. When we think logically, we have images in our conceptions and ideas. But these images are only inner thought-forms, just as the forms of a statue are forms.

Now the spiritual investigator sets out from this mode of thinking. In my books, *Knowledge of the Higher Worlds*, and *Stages of Higher Knowledge*, directions are to be found as to what must be done with thinking in order that it may become something entirely different from what it is in ordinary life and ordinary science. The spiritual investigator develops his thinking, he makes it undergo a certain special discipline. I cannot in this short sketch enter into details, these are described in the books I have named. When thinking, when the logic that bears sway in man, is treated in a certain way, the whole inner life of the soul becomes changed. Something happens which changes this soul-life into something else, which I will once more make clear by a comparison.

Imagine that the statue—this, of course, cannot happen, but let us assume that it could—imagine that the statue, which previously stood there with its lifeless form, were suddenly to begin to walk and to become living. This the statue cannot do ; but human think-ing, inner logical activity, can. By means of the soul-exercises undertaken and carried out by the spiritual investigator, he puts himself into such a state, that there is within him not only a thought-out logic, but a living logic ; logic itself becomes a *living being* within him. Thereby he has grasped something living and bearing sway within him, instead of lifeless conceptions. He becomes permeated by this living, ruling element. And when spiritual research assumes the existence of an etheric body, besides the physical body which is visible to bodily eyes, by this is meant not something merely imagined, but it is meant that man, by bringing logical thinking to life within him, becomes conscious of a second human being within him. This is a matter of experience which may be arrived at. The experience must be made, in order that the science of the spiritual human being may arise, just as the outer experiments of natural science must be made, in order to learn nature's secrets.

Just as thinking is so transformed that it no longer leads merely to images, but becomes inwardly active and alive, so may the will also be developed in a certain way. The methods by which the will is so treated that we learn to know it as something different from what it is in ordinary life, are also to be found

described in the above-named books. Through
this development of the will, something of
quite a different kind results from what comes
through the development of thinking. If we
desire to do something in ordinary life, if we
work, the will, as it were, penetrates into the
limbs. We say, " I will " ; we move our
hands ; but the will only comes to expression
in this movement. In its real essence it remains
unknown. But by using certain exercises, the
will may be released from its connection with
the limbs. The will may be experienced in
itself alone. Thinking may be made active, so
as to become something inwardly alive, a kind
of etheric body. The will may be isolated,
separated from its connection with the bodily
nature, and then we realise that we have
within us a second human being in a far higher
sense than is the case with thinking. Through
the development of the will we become aware
that we have a second human being within us,
which has a consciousness of its own. If we
work at our will in an adequate way, something takes place which I can only make clear
by reminding you that in ordinary human life
there are two alternating states, waking life
and sleep. In waking life man lives consciously ; during sleep, consciousness ceases.

Now at first it is a mere assertion to say
that the soul and spirit do not cease to be conscious between the time of falling asleep and

awaking. But they are no longer directly in the body, they are outside it. The spiritual investigator succeeds in voluntarily giving his bodily life the same form that it takes involuntarily when he goes to sleep. He orders his senses and his ordinary intellect to be still ; he achieves this by developing his will. And it then happens that the same condition is voluntarily brought about that is usually involuntarily present in sleep. Yet, on the other hand, what is now brought about is the complete opposite of the sleep-condition. Whereas during sleep we become unconscious and know nothing about ourselves and our surroundings, through developing the will in the manner described we consciously leave our bodies ; we see the body outside ourselves, just as we usually perceive an external object outside ourselves. Then we notice that in man there lives a real spectator of his thoughts and actions. This is no mere image, no merely pictorial expression, but it is a reality. In our will there lives something which is perpetually observing us inwardly. It is easy to look upon this inner spectator as something intended to be taken pictorially ; the spiritual investigator knows it to be a reality, just as the objects of sense are realities. And if we have these two, the living, moving thought-being, the etheric human being, and this inner spectator, then we have brought ourselves into a spiritual world, which is actually experienced, as the physical world is experienced with the senses. A second human being is found in man in this way, as oxygen is found in water by the methods of natural science.

That which is attained by developed thinking, is not visions, but spiritual sight of realities; what is attained by a developed will, is not ordinary soul-experiences, but the discovery of a different consciousness from the ordinary one. There now act one upon the other, the human being who is logic in motion, and the other human being who is a higher consciousness. If we learn to know these two within man, we know that part of man which exists even when his physical body falls into decay, when he goes through the gate of death. We learn to know the being in man which does not act through the outer body, which is of a soul and spirit nature, which will continue to exist after death, which existed also before birth, or, let us say, before conception. We learn to know the eternal essence of man in this way, through having separated it, as it were, out of the ordinary mortal human being, just as we can separate oxygen out of water by a chemical process.

All that I have now brought before you must of course still be looked upon as fantastic at the present time ; in relation to customary ideas, it is as fantastic as the words of Coperni-

cus seemed, when he said, " It is not the
sun which revolves round the earth, but the
earth revolves round the sun." Nevertheless,
what appears so fantastic is really only something unaccustomed. It is not the case that
something invented or dreamed has been
related in what has just been set forth, but the
point is that the spiritual is actually experienced
as a fact by means of inward processes. The
spiritual investigator is not speaking in a simple
manner of man's nature when he enumerates,
" Man consists of a physical body, etheric
body, astral body, etc.," but he is showing how
that which is human nature, when it is con-
templated as a whole, becomes split up into
certain principles of which it is composed.
And if the matter be regarded in accordance
with its fundamental essence, nothing magical
or mystical in a bad sense is meant by these
principles of man's being. Spiritual science
shows that man consists of different gradations,
different shades of human nature. And this in
a higher sphere is no different from the fact,
in a lower one, that light may be so treated as
to appear in seven colours. Just as light must
be split up into seven colours in order that it
may be studied, so must man be divided into
his several parts in order that he may be really
studied.

It should not be expected that what is
spiritual can be brought before bodily eyes,

before the senses. It must be experienced inwardly and spiritually. And to one who will not admit that inward experience, a spiritual experience, is in any way a fact, anything said by the spiritual investigator will be but empty skirmishing with words. To one who learns to know spiritual facts, these are realities in a far higher sense than are physical facts. If a plant grows, and develops blossom and fruit, a new plant again develops out of the seed; and when we have learned to know the germ, we know that it has the full force of the plant within it, and that a new plant arises from the germ.

What is of the nature of spirit and soul must be learned from facts belonging to the spirit and soul; then we know that in the living thought, which is apprehended by the consciousness that is liberated out of the will, a life-germ has been discerned, which passes through the gate of death, goes through the spiritual world after death and afterwards returns again to earth-life. And just as truly as the plant-seed develops a new plant, does that which is the kernel of man's being develop a new earth-life. This new human being can be seen in the present one, for it becomes inwardly alive.

Natural science has methods of calculating certain events which will happen in the future. From the relative positions of the sun and

4

moon it may be calculated when eclipses of
these will occur. It is only necessary to know
the corresponding factors in order to calculate
when a certain conjunction of the stars will
take place. In these cases it is necessary to
use mathematics, because we are dealing with
external space. The life-germ, which is inwardly experienced, also contains in a living
way the indication of future earth-lives. Just
as future eclipses of the sun and moon are
indicated in the present relations of those
bodies, so are future earth-lives indicated in
that which is now alive within us. In this case
we are not dealing with what, according to
more ancient views, is called the transmigra-
tion of souls, but with something which modern
spiritual research discovers from the facts of
spiritual life, wh.ch are capable of being
investigated.

Now certain things must be carefully kept
in view if we wish to understand the real
foundations of spiritual research. We arrive
at leaving the body with our soul and spirit
through treating thought and will in the
manner that has been indicated. We are then
outside the body ; and just as we usually have
outer things before our eyes, so do we have our
own physical body before us. But the essential
thing is that we can *always* observe this body.
And if it is a case of spiritual research in the
true sense of the words, as it is here meant,

that must never happen which does so in a diseased soul-life. For what is the characteristic feature of an abnormal or diseased soul-life ? If some one is put into a hypnotic state or a so-called trance, as certain conditions are called, and speaks out of the subconscious, which is often denominated a kind of clairvoyance, the essential thing in the process is that the ordinary consciousness is not present whilst the changed consciousness is active. The former has been transformed into a dulled, abnormal consciousness. It will never be possible to say, when observing an abnormal and unhealthy condition of soul, " The healthy condition of soul is present at the same time as this," for in that case the person would certainly not be unhealthy or abnormal.

In real spiritual research the fact is that man arrives at a changed consciousness, but that as a normal human being he is all the time standing by. The condition in which the spiritual investigator is, is not developed *from out of* ordinary normal soul-life, but *by the side of it*, if the condition is the right one. In the case of a genuine spiritual investigator, he lives, during his researches, outside his body ; but his body continues to work on undisturbed together with all his normal soul-functions and his ordinary intellect, which remains completely normal. The man, if he is a true spiritual investigator, remains a normal human being, in spite of the fact that he has left his body, together with what he has developed within himself; and one who cannot himself investigate spiritually, really need not see that the other is living in a different world. The non-hypnotised person is not present beside the hypnotised one, the person with a normal soul-life is not present beside the one who is developing an abnormal soul-life. But the characteristic feature of spiritual research is that whilst it is being pursued, the person's normal condition is completely maintained. Just on this account the spiritual investigator is in a position accurately to distinguish true spiritual research from that which appears in any diseased conditions of soul.

Another mistake arises when it is thought that spiritual research has anything in common with ordinary spiritualism. By this it is not meant that all manner of facts may not be discovered through spiritualism, but these belong to natural science, not to spiritual science, for that which is discovered through spiritualism is presented to the outer senses, whether by means of materialisations, or knockings and the like. That which can be presented to the senses belongs to natural science. That which offers itself as an object to the spiritual investigator is of a soul and spirit nature, and cannot be presented externally, for instance, in space; it must be experienced inwardly.

Through the inner experience which has been described there is formed a comprehensive spiritual science, which not only throws light on the being of man and the passage through repeated earth-lives, but is also enlightening about the spiritual worlds and spiritual beings which lie behind nature. Spiritual research is able to enter the world through which man passes after death. Only it must not be thought that what appear in ordinary life in a certain sense as abnormal faculties have any special value in spiritual science. There is much talk nowadays of the possibility of telepathy. We will not now enter into all the pros and cons of this matter. People must grow accustomed to many things in the course of time. Just at the present time serious investigators are wrestling with the problem of the significance of the divining-rod, which is now so widely used, and about which one of the most matter-of-fact investigators is just now making important experiments, in order to ascertain what influence a person is under who is successful with the divining-rod. But all this belongs to the department of finer natural science. In the same way does the fact belong to this department that thoughts entertained by one person are able to influence another at a distance. True spiritual research cannot use such forces for gaining knowledge about the world of soul and spirit. It is a

complete misunderstanding of spiritual science
to think that it looks upon the teaching about
telepathy as anything else but a part of a
refined physiology, a refined form of natural
science.

The way in which spiritual science investi-
gates must not be confused with that which
nowadays appears as spiritualism. When
spiritual science remembers the human souls
which are passing through a purely spiritual
life in a spiritual world between death and
re-birth, spiritual science knows that those
souls are in the spiritual world in a soul-state
pure and simple. Now it is possible for the
spirit and soul that is in a human body to turn
to the dead in such a way that a real connection is made with them. But this turning
to the dead must itself be of a purely spiritual
and soul character. Spiritual science shows
this. And the direction of our own soul-life to
our beloved dead may acquire deep significance, even whilst we ourselves are still in the
physical world. It cannot be at variance with
any religious belief if, through the view of the
world taken by spiritual science, remembrance
of the dead and active communion with them
is cultivated in this way, if spiritual science
stimulates this living together with the dead.
In this connection it must always be borne in
mind that the dead person can only be aware
of what we are thinking and feeling for him

in our souls if he *desires* such a connection
with us. This also is shown by spiritual
science. The exercise of any sort of power
over the dead is entirely remote from the
intentions of the spiritual investigator. He
knows quite well that the dead are living in a
sphere in which the relations of the will are
different from those in the physical world ; and
if he were to wish to penetrate into the spiritual
world, taking with him what he is able to
develop here within the physical world, it
would seem to him as though—to use a comparison—a company of people were sitting
here and a lion suddenly appeared through the
floor and committed ravages. So would harm
result if an earthly human being were to force
his way into the life of the dead in an un-
befitting manner. Therefore there can be
no question in spiritual science of summoning
the dead, in the way in which this is attempted
in spiritualism, just because the relations of
the living to the dead are illuminated in a
wonderful way by that which spiritual science
arouses within our souls. And since amongst
the numerous errors which have been urged
against our spiritual science, one is that it has
a connection with spiritualism with regard to
the dead, it is very necessary to emphasise this
misunderstanding sharply. Nothing less than
the exact *contrary of the truth* is asserted with
regard to spiritual science in this matter.

As already said, I do not wish to proselytise or arouse feeling for our cause, but only to mention misunderstandings which I know to be prevalent, and to indicate in the clearest way possible the relation of spiritual science to these matters.

Now the question is also asked—and it is even called an urgent one—What is the position of spiritual science or Anthroposophy towards the religious life of man? Its very nature, however, prevents it from interposing directly in any religious confession, in the sphere of any religious life. In this connection I can perhaps make myself clear in the following way. Let us assume that we have to do with natural science. Because we gain a knowledge of nature, we shall not imagine that we are able to create something in nature itself. Knowledge of nature does not create anything in nature. Nor, because we gain knowledge of spiritual conditions, shall we imagine that we are able to create something in spiritual facts. We observe spiritual conditions. Spiritual science endeavours to penetrate behind the mysteries of the spiritual conditions in the world. Religions are facts in the historical life of humanity. Spiritual science can of course go so far as to consider the spiritual phenomena which have appeared as religions in the course of the world's evolution. But spiritual science can never

desire to create a religion, any more than
natural science surrenders itself to the illusion
of being able to create something in nature.
Hence the most various religious confessions
will be able to live together in the profoundest
peace, and in complete harmony within the
circle of the view of the world taken by spiritual
science, and will be able to strive together after
knowledge of the spiritual—so to strive that
the religious convictions of the individual will
not thereby be in any way injured. Neither
need intensity in the exercise of a religious
belief be in any way lessened by what is found
in spiritual science. Rather must it be said
that natural science, as it has appeared in
modern times, has very often led people away
from a religious conception of life, from the
exercise of true, inner religion. It is an experience which we have in spiritual science that
people who have been alienated from all
religious life by the half-truths of natural
science can be brought back again to that life
through spiritual science. No one need be in
any way estranged from his religious life
through spiritual science. For this reason it
cannot be said that spiritual science, as such,
is a religious belief. It desires neither to create
a religious belief, nor to change a man in any
way with regard to the religious belief which
he holds. Nevertheless it seems as though
people were talking about the religion of the

Anthroposophists ! In reality such a thing
cannot be said, for all religious beliefs are
represented within the Anthroposophical
Society ; and no one is prevented by it from
practically exercising his religious belief in the
fullest, most comprehensive and most intense
way. It is only that spiritual science desires
to include the whole world in its survey ; it
desires to survey historical life, together with
the highest spirituality which has entered
historical life. That for this reason it also
takes a survey of religions is absolutely no contradiction of what I have just said. And thus
it comes to pass that the view of the world
taken by spiritual science must in a certain
respect deepen a man, even with regard to the
objects of religious life.

But when, for instance, it happens that
spiritual science is accused of not speaking
of a personal God, when it is said that I
prefer to speak of the Divinity, not of God,
when it is asserted that what is called " the
divine " in spiritual science is of a similar
nature to that which is so designated in the
pantheism of the Monists or Naturalists, this
is all the opposite of the truth. Through the
very circumstance that in spiritual science
we are led to real spiritual beings, and to the
real being that man is after death, just because
we are led to concrete, real spiritual beings,
we arrive at being able completely to under-

stand how unreasonable it is to become a
pantheist, how repugnant to common sense to
deny personality in God. One arrives, on the
contrary, at seeing that one may speak not
only of the personality, but even of a super-
personality of God. The most thorough
refutation of pantheism may be found through
spiritual science.

Can it be a subject of reproach that the
spiritual investigator only speaks with deep
reverence when, out of the feelings which his
knowledge arouses in him, he points the way
with awe to the divine ? How often it is said
in the circle of our friends, " In Him we live,
and move, and have our being." And one
who wishes to comprehend God with one idea,
does not know that all possible ideas cannot
comprehend God, because all ideas are *in* God.
But the recognition of God as a being who
has personality in a much higher sense even
than man, in a sense which even through
spiritual science cannot be fully perceived,
becomes quite, I would say, natural to people,
specially through Anthroposophy. Religious
conceptions are not made misty, in the pantheistic sense, through spiritual science, but,
in accordance with their nature, become
deepened. If we say that God is revealed in
our own hearts and souls, this is surely the
conviction of many religious people ; and it is
again and again said in spiritual science that

there can be no question in this of wishing to deify man.

I have often used the simile that a drop taken out of the sea is water—do I therefore say that the drop is the sea? If I say that something divine speaks in the individual human soul, a drop out of the ocean of the infinite divine, do I therefore say anything which deifies the individual human soul? Do I say anything which unites nature with God in a pantheistic way? Far from it. And finally, if from certain deeply seated feelings which are aroused by spiritual science itself, the name "GOD" is, in reverential awe, not named but paraphrased, should this be a subject of blame from the religious point of view? I ask, is not one of the Ten Commandments, "Thou shalt not take the name of the Lord thy God in vain"? May not spiritual science stimulate to a faithful fulfilment of this command, if the name of God is not perpetually on the lips of its followers?

And the name and being of Christ? It is just of spiritual science that it may be said that it makes every effort to understand the being of Christ, and that in doing so it is never at variance with that which is developed, from true foundations, by any religious denomination. Only, in this very domain, we meet with something most singular. Some one comes and says he has a certain conception or feeling about Christ, about Jesus, and we say to him, " Certainly, we recognise these feelings as wholly justified ; only spiritual science leads to thinking many other things about Christ as well. It does not deny what you say, it accepts it. Only it must add much more to it."

Just because spiritual science widens the spiritual sight, the eye of the soul, to extend over the spiritual world, is it necessary not only to recognise in the being to whom the Christian looks up as his Christ, the one who walked this earth, but to bring this being into connection with the entire cosmos. And then, again, much else is the consequence of so doing. But nothing which results from it takes anything away from the knowledge of Christ, only something is added to what the religious man, the really Christian religious man, has to say about the Christ. And when some one attacks the conception of Christ Jesus held by spiritual science, it always seems to the spiritual investigator as though some one comes and says, " I have this or that to say about the Christ ; do you believe it ? "   " Yes ! "   we say. " Yes, but you not only believe that, but more besides ! ". This he will not allow. He is not satisfied with our admitting what he advocates, but he forbids us to declare something still greater and grander about the Christ than he himself declares.

For can it really be a heresy when spiritual

science, out of its fundamental basis, out of
the observation of that which, as spirit, holds
sway through the whole progress of the earth
with regard to human and other evolution,
arrives at saying, " The whole existence of the
earth would have no meaning in the universe
if the Mystery of Golgotha had not taken place
within the earthly sphere " ?   The spiritual
investigator must say, " If any inhabitants of
distant worlds could look down upon the earth
and see what it is, they would see no meaning
in the whole evolution of the earth unless
Christ had lived, died and risen again upon it."
The event of Golgotha gives meaning and
purpose to earth-life for the whole world.
If you were to study the results of spiritual
research, you would see that reverence for
Christ and devotion to Him cannot be diminished by such research, but on the contrary
can only be enhanced.

Time presses, and I cannot enter into many
other misunderstandings which have been
spread abroad concerning certain thoughts
about the Bible which are said to be prevalent
in circles of Anthroposophists—as they are
called, although the word would be better
avoided, and only " Anthroposophy " used.
The point in this case is that a person may be
a very good spiritual investigator without in
any way being able to accept what has, for
definite reasons, been said for those members

of our society who wish to know something
about the Gospels or the Bible generally. But
if what is said be read with the context, it will
be found that, for instance, I never uttered
such nonsense as that repeated earth - lives
could be proved from the Bible by means of
the passage in which Nathanael is spoken of.
It has been asserted that I thought that when
the Christ says, " When thou wast under the
fig-tree, I saw thee," he is referring to an
earlier incarnation, in which he saw Nathanael
sitting under the fig-tree. I can do but one
thing when these misunderstandings fly about
the world to-day, I can do but one thing—
wonder how such things have been able to
arise at all out of what was really said. They
are just proofs of the manner in which what is
really said becomes altered in the most diverse
ways when it is repeated from one to another,
and how the contrary—for in this case it is
the contrary that came out—of what I had
said was attributed to me.

I will not now discuss other misunderstandings, which could easily be refuted. I will only
mention one thing, which may very easily be
said, " What do you think of the fact that
nothing about repeated earth-lives is found in
the Bible ? " It might be that some one would
say that he could not believe in these repeated
earth-lives, for the simple reason that, according to his convictions, there is a contradiction

between the acceptation of these repeated earth-lives, which, certainly, minds such as Lessing's, for instance, admitted as true, and what is in the Bible.

Now repeated earth-lives will be accepted as a scientific, a spiritually scientific fact, and people will learn to think in the following way about the relation to the Bible of such a fact of spiritual science, which had sooner or later to be discovered. Would it be thought possible for anyone to say he did not believe in the existence of America because the Bible does not mention such a place? Or would it be thought any injury to the Bible to say, " I think the existence of America is quite in harmony with my reverence for the Bible, in spite of America's not being mentioned within its pages " ? Is there anything in the Bible about the truth of the Copernican view of the universe? There have been people who for this reason have looked upon the Copernican view of the world as something false and forbidden. Nowadays there is no one really versed in the culture of his time who could say that he found a contradiction between the teaching of Copernicus and the Bible—notwithstanding that the teaching of Copernicus is not in the Bible.

In the same way it may be said of the spiritually scientific fact of repeated earth-lives that there is no injury done to the cardinal

truths of the Bible, merely because nothing
can be found therein about reincarnation, and
because, indeed, much of its contents may be
so interpreted as to seem to contradict this
knowledge.   These points must only be looked
at from the right point of view.   If they are
so looked at, it may very well be remembered
how such things change in the course of time.
If some one says he will not admit the truth
of repeated earth-lives for the reason that it
contradicts the Bible, I am always reminded
that there was a time when Galileo was treated
in a very peculiar, well-known way, because
he had something to say which apparently,
but only apparently, contradicted the Bible.
Or we may remember how Giordano Bruno
was treated, because he too had something
to say about which it was asserted that
it could not be demonstrated out of the
Bible.

I must, moreover, remember a priest who
became the rector of a university some years
ago, from the theological faculty, and who in
his rectorial address, the subject of which was
Galileo, spoke as a Catholic priest somewhat
as follows.   He said that times change, and
with them the way in which people accept
recognised facts.   Galileo was in his time
treated as we all know ; but now every true
Christian sees that through the discovery of
the grandeur of the cosmic system, as it

became known through Galileo, the glory and
majesty of God and devotion to Him can only
be increased, not diminished. This was like
a priest, it was like a Christian, indeed it was
perhaps said for the first time in a really
Christian way. And the fine recognition of
Galileo was Christian, which was gained for
him from the whole address of this priest.

On the whole I would say, speaking from
the convictions of spiritual science, that the
spiritual scientist must, through his teachings,
so think of what Christianity is, and of what
Christ is to the world, as to say, " How faint-
hearted are those who think that in consequence of some discovery in the physical or
spiritual domain the greatness which breathes .
towards us from the revelation of Christ can
be diminished." To the spiritual investigator
he seems faint-hearted who thinks that through
some fact, even such a weighty one as repeated
earth-lives, some fact which is discovered in
the physical or spiritual sphere, the splendour
of the Christ-event and the influence of Christ
can be lessened to the Christian ; one who
believes this might also believe that the sun
loses power because it does not shine only for
Europe, but for America too.

Whatever further physical or spiritual facts
may be discovered, in any far-distant future,
the great truths of Christianity will outshine
them all. This is discerned by one who ap-

proaches the Christ-impulse and the enti e
Christian conception of the world with the
attitude of spiritual research.   Such an one has
no fear.   He is not so faint-hearted as to say
that the splendour of Christianity can be
diminished by any investigation.   He knows
that one who believes that Christianity can be
imperilled by any physical or spiritual research,
does not think much of Christianity.

It is really a question whether perhaps the
numerous misunderstandings which exist with
regard to that for which the Dornach building
is an outward sign, an outer home, can be
overcome.   About the Dornach building itself
I will only say to-day that it is intended to be
nothing else but an artistic putting into form
of that which is aroused in our perceptions
and feelings when we have received into our
souls the living essence of spiritual science or
Anthroposophy.   Therefore it should not be
thought that the ideas of spiritual science are
pictured by means of symbols or allegories in
the forms of the building.   Of that there is no
question at all.

If you visit this building you will find that
it has the peculiarity of having nothing at all
mysterious in it, not a single symbol, nothing
allegorical or the like.   This has, from the very
nature of the building, been kept entirely
remote from it.

It may perhaps be said, " But it is necessary

to know the thoughts belonging to spiritual science in order to understand what one sees ! " This is true, but it is what the art of the Dornach building has in common with every other art. Take the Sistine Madonna, the wonderful picture of the Mother with the Child Jesus. I think that if a person who had never heard anything about Christianity were to stand before the Sistine Madonna, it would be necessary to explain to him what it is, for he too would not be able to understand the subject out of his own feelings. Thus it is a matter of course that it is necessary to live quite in the current of spiritual science in order to understand its art, just as it is necessary to be in the midst of Christianity in order to understand the Sistine Madonna.

The attempt is not made, in the Dornach building, to express the ideas of spiritual science symbolically, but there underlies it this fact of our view of the world, namely, that spiritual science is something—and this follows from what I have said here to-day—which takes hold of man's inner being in such a living, powerful way, that faculties otherwise dormant in him — artistic faculties as well as others—are awakened. And as spiritual science is something new—not a new name for something old, but something really new— just as present-day natural science is new as compared with the natural science of the

Middle Ages, its art too must be something new and different from existing works of art. Gothic art came forward as new, compared with the antique ; anyone who is of opinion that only antique art is of value may despise the Gothic ; in the same way may a new style be abused, which arises out of a new way of feeling.

An accessory building is found specially bad. Near the building with two domes stands a heating-house. The attempt has been made to construct a useful building artistically out of the most modern of materials, concrete. The concrete was taken into account. And on the other hand everything that is in the building was taken into account. If anyone explains the form emblematically, if he sees all kinds of symbols in it, he is just a dreamer, a visionary, not one who sees what is there. Just as a nutshell is shaped so as to fit the nut-kernel, so does the artist try, in what he constructs, to form a shell for what is within it, a shell as it were in conformity with nature, so that the outer form is the appropriate covering of what it contains. That is what is attempted. And one who criticises this building and does not think it beautful can be understood, for one must first grow used to these things. But he might perhaps try to imagine another chimney, as chimneys are now built, beside our heating-house, a correct, red chimney with its ordinary surroundings ; and he might then compare the two.

It is true we very well know that what is attempted in the building at Dornach is but a beginning, and an imperfect beginning, but it is intended as the beginning of something which is arising out of a new view of the world, as a new style of architecture. There are also people who said, " Look, you have made seven columns, seven on each side of the principal hall. You are a very superstitious society ; you believe in the mystical number seven."

Well, one who sees seven colours in the rainbow might also be thought superstitious. In that case it is really nature, which causes the fact, which should be thought superstitious. But anyone who talks about these seven columns should not at first consider the number, but consider what has been newly attempted in the matter. Elsewhere, similar columns are placed near each other. The capitals of our columns are designed to be in continuous development ; the second column is different from the first, the third again different ; one capital arises out of another. This results in an organism, which has inner laws in the same way as have the seven tones, from the tonic to the leading note.

It will thus be found that nowhere have ideas, symbolism or the mysterious been elaborated, but the endeavour has everywhere been made to develop something artistic in forms, colours and so forth. We have striven to make the whole building the right framework for what is to be carried on within it. Buildings have walls. In walls as they have hitherto been built, people are accustomed to see something so framed as to shut off space. Our walls are so covered over with forms from inside that there is no feeling of space being shut off by the form, but one has the feeling that the wall is pervious and that one is looking out into the infinite. The walls are so constructed in their forms that they seem to efface themselves, and we remain in connection with nature and the whole world.

In this short account I have not wished to convince anyone. I wished to do only what I laid stress on at the beginning ; I wish to interest, not to convince. But one thing I would fain emphasise once more—the way in which people become conversant with a particular view of the world depends on their habits of thought. And one who is acquainted with the course taken by the spiritual evolution of mankind knows that truth has always had to be developed through obstacles. Only consider how Giordano Bruno had to come forth before humanity, a humanity which had always believed that the blue vault of heaven was the limit of space. Giordano Bruno had to tell people, " There is nothing at all where

you see the blue vault of the sky ; you put
something there yourselves when you look at
it.   Space stretches out into infinity, and
infinite worlds are in the infinite space."
What Giordano Bruno then did for physical
observation, spiritual science has to do for soul
and spirit, and for what is temporal.   In regard
to soul and spirit there is also a kind of firmament, on one side birth, or let us say conception, on the other side, death.   But that
firmament is actually just as little a reality
as the blue firmament above ; merely because
people can only see as far as birth or conception and as far as death with ordinary
human faculties of perception, they think
there is a boundary there, as people used to
think the firmament was a boundary.   But
just as the blue firmament is no boundary, but
infinite worlds exist in infinite space, so must
we, with enlarged faculties, look out beyond
the firmament of birth and death into an
infinity of time, and behold in it the development of the eternal soul throughout successive
earth-lives.   In the spiritual sphere things are
not different from what they are in the sphere
of natural science.   Therefore it may be asked :
How is it then that so many misunderstandings
arise from so many quarters about spiritual
science ?   In this case I must say, if I may
treat the matter more or less personally, that
I think the reasons why spiritual science meets

with so much hostility and misunderstanding
are partly objective and partly subjective.

Amongst the objective reasons I would place
this one first and foremost : Spiritual science
is something upon which it is necessary to
concentrate one's thoughts seriously.   Long
and earnest work is needful in order to understand it, work which is inseparable from many
experiences and even from many disappoint-
ments.   But this is in reality the case with
every subject of knowledge.   The paths of
Anthroposophy cannot be found without such
work.   It seems to be the custom to say that
for the understanding of a watch it is necessary to learn how the wheels work together.
This demands some trouble.   But it does
not seem to be equally customary to make
a similar admission with regard to the universe
at large.   In this case difficult, apparently
complicated views are not allowed to have
any value, and yet they are only difficult
because the subject in hand is so.   Instead
of studying spiritual science themselves, people
find fault with it because, judged from their
own point of view, it is difficult.

Then there are subjective reasons.   And
these are to be found in what I have already
said.   It is difficult for people in general to
reconcile ideas which they have once formed
with ideas to which they are unaccustomed.
Such unaccustomed ideas need not even

contradict those already entertained, but need only add something to what has already been thought.

It has always been thus with truth. What is contradicted is people's habits of thought. And from this point of view, if the subjective reasons for misunderstandings about spiritual science are sought, we must say that the reasons are to be found on the same ground from which the teaching of Copernicus was rejected by the whole world, when it first appeared. It was just something new. But truth has to make its own way in the world, and does so in the end. This may well be felt by one who has at heart spiritual science, and all that to which it stimulates.

He relies on the experience that truth always works its way through the smallest crevices in the rocks of prejudices which have been set up. Perhaps spiritual science may still be hated now. But one who hates it will, at the most, only be able to make others hate it with him, people who are attached to him and swear by what he says. But never yet has a truth been effaced through having been hated. Truth may at any time be misunderstood and misinterpreted, but there will always be found those who know* and rightly understand, in the face of those who misconstrue and misjudge. And even if that which spiritual science has to say in our time is not now recognised as true,

if it is misunderstood and unappreciated, the
time will come for this science also. Truth
may be suppressed, but not destroyed. It must
always be born again, however often it may
be suppressed.

For truth is intimately, deeply and vitally
bound up with the human soul, in such a way
that one may be convinced that the human
soul and truth belong to one another like
sisters. And even if there are times and places
in which dissension comes about between them,
and some misunderstanding arises, recognition
and mutual love must always reappear between
the soul and truth. For they are sisters, who
have a common origin, and must always be
lovingly mindful of their common origin—
their origin in the spirituality which rules
throughout the universe, and the discovery
of which is the very task which Anthroposophy
sets itself.

AFTERWORD

BY means of the details given in this booklet, it was to be shown how anthroposophical spiritual science receives its form at the present time as knowledge of the spiritual world, by going along lines which can hold their own by the side of the authorised lines of a scientific way of looking at things. In order to penetrate into the spiritual world in just as trustworthy a manner as natural science does into the world of matter, spiritual science must take paths which are different from those of natural science. In order to satisfy in a spiritual sphere the same demands which natural science satisfies in its sphere, it must work with faculties of perception and knowledge which are adapted to the spiritual, just as those of natural science are adapted to nature. A spiritual science with aims such as these cannot in any way be confused with more ancient tendencies of thought such as the Gnosis, etc. We can observe how in the course of modern times the effort to arrive at it appears quite clearly. Therefore it does not come forth as something which is voluntarily fabricated at the present time, but as the fulfilment of hopes which can be observed in the mental development of the West. Many things might be adduced to prove this; but we will only give two examples here, which show that " Anthroposophy " is something that has been thought about for a long time. *Troxler*, a thinker of the first half of the nineteenth century who is much under-estimated, published his *Vorlesungen über Philosophie* in 1835. In this work there is the sentence, " Although it is highly gratifying that the latest philosophy . . . winds upwards in every *Anthroposophy*, i.e., it must be revealed in poetry as well as in history, we must not overlook the fact that this idea cannot be the fruit of speculation, and the true personality or individuality of man may not be confused either with what it sets up as subjective spirit or final ego, or with what it contrasts with this as absolute spirit or absolute personality." What Troxler brings forward regarding his idea of Anthroposophy is confined to statements which clearly show how close he is to the acceptance of principles of human nature beyond the physical body. He says, " In earlier times philosophers differentiated a delicate, sublime soul-body from the grosser body. This they considered to be a sort of vehicle of the spirit, and it was an image of the body. They called it the *pattern*, and looked upon it as the inner, higher man." The connection in which these words are found in Troxler's work, and the whole of his conception of the world, testify that we may see in his case aspirations which are fulfilled in the spiritual science indicated in this booklet. Only, as Troxler is not in the position to recognise that Anthroposophy is only possible through the development of soul-capacities in the direction indicated in this booklet, his own views relapse to points of view which, as compared with those attained by J. G. Fichte, Schelling and Hegel are not an advance, but a retrogression. (See my book *Die Rätsel der Philosophie*.) In the work of J. H. Fichte, the son of the great philosopher, viz., in his *Anthropologie*, second edition 1860, page 608, we find the following sentences, " Anthropology ends in the result which is confirmed from various quarters, that the true nature of man's being and the real source of his consciousness belong to a supersensible world. But sense-consciousness and the phenomenal world which appears before his eyes, together with the whole of the life of the senses, have no other importance than merely to be the place where that supersensible life of the spirit is realised, by his bringing the spiritual contents of ideas into the sense-world *through his own free, conscious act.* . . . The final result of this fundamental comprehension

of human nature raises ' Anthropology ' to
' *Anthroposophy.*' " In connection with the
explanation of these sentences J. H. Fichte
says (p. 609), " Thus, finally, Anthroposophy
itself is only able to find its final conclusion in
Theosophy." The reasons why J. H. Fichte
with his own view of the world did not arrive
at Anthroposophy, but fell behind J. G.
Fichte, Schelling and Hegel, are the same
as in Troxler's case. For the present we will
only give these two examples out of a multi-
tude of facts contained in the history of the
spiritual development of mankind, which could
be adduced to prove that the anthroposophical
spiritual science characterised in this booklet
responds to a scientific tendency which has
existed for a long time.

*   *   *

In a lecture which I gave in 1902 before the
Giordano Bruno Union, I referred to these
statements by J. H. Fichte (which seemed to
me to be the expression of a modern intellectual movement, not merely of an individual
opinion) ; that was the time when a beginning
was made with what now appears as the
anthroposophical way of looking at things.
From this it may be seen that we had in view
the extension of the modern tendency of
thought to the genuine observation of spiritual

reality. We did not try to bring forth certain
views out of the publications then called
" theosophical " (and still so named at the
present time), but we strove to continue the
aspirations given birth to by modern philosophers, aspirations which, however, in their
case remained in abstractions, and thus did
not gain entrance to the true spiritual world.
At the same time, this continuation seemed
to me to be an extension of the view which
Goethe, placing it at the foundation of his
view of nature, which he described as being
" in accordance with the spirit," did not
actually express, but *felt*. One who has
followed my writings and lectures may gather
all this from them ; and I would not specially
mention this matter if the misrepresentation
of the truth were not brought up again and
again, when it is said that I have changed
from all that I wrote and said formerly and
have turned to the views represented in the
works of Blavatsky and Besant. One who
carefully studies, for example, my *Theosophy*,
will find that everything contained in it is
developed in accordance with and as a continuation of the above-described direction of
modern thought ; he will find that the matters
dealt with are presented in accordance with
certain presuppositions contained in Goethe's
conception of the world, and that only in
certain places is it mentioned that ideas which

I had arrived at (etheric body, sensation body, etc.), are also to be found in literature which is called theosophical. I know that by these explanations I shall not be able to do away with certain attacks made against me again and again, for in many cases these attacks are not made in order to arrive at the actual facts of the matter, but for something entirely different. But what can be done in the face of ever-recurring inexactitudes? Nothing can be done but to reiterate the truth!

*   *   *

The searcher who works on the basis of the kind of knowledge indicated in this booklet sees that the method of his investigations is in complete accord with the endeavours of present-day natural science. But he knows that these endeavours of natural science must everywhere come to a standstill or run into blind alleys if they do not meet what spiritual science can bring to light from opposite starting-points. A true view of the matter would look upon both directions of work as being like the boring of a tunnel, which commences from opposite directions, but, when the work is properly arranged, the two parties meet. The *facts* of contemporary work fully confirm this view. It is only misled opinions regarding these facts which deny this and presume that spiritual science and natural science contradict each other. This contradiction, however, does not really exist. We have a brilliant example of the importance of the meeting of natural science and spiritual science in a book which has just been published, in my opinion an epoch-making book. *Vom Schaltwerk der Gedanken : Neue Einsichten und Betrachtungen über die Seele*, by *Karl Ludwig Schleich*. If you read the important chapter on "Hysteria—a metaphysical problem," you will see how a practical physician, who is at the same time a penetrating thinker, confronts facts which can only be fully elucidated by spiritual science, facts which compel him to say, "In the production of tissue through the impulse of hysteria we have the metaphysical problem of incarnation," in "mediumistic vision, a kind of clairvoyance of possibilities of disease." But a person would be under one of the very worst of illusions if he seriously thought that without the results of spiritual science he could explain all the actual experiences of man by the facts discovered by natural science. The scientist who refuses to consider spiritual science is like a man who has a piece of magnetic iron in his hand, but has no notion of magnetism and only uses the iron for an instrument in which magnetism plays no part. What would have come out of it if he had put the magnetism and not the material iron to some use ? If you

also read in Schleich's book the chapter on
" The myth of the change of matter in the
brain," you will see for yourself how, by con-
straint of thought, the scientific physician
comes to a formal description of what spiritual
science—from a comprehensive presentation
of spirit-life—appropriately describes as the
etheric body of man.   It is interesting to notice
how this particular chapter in Schleich's book
shows that at the present time natural science
and spiritual science often talk in vain, because
the co-operation of natural scientists and
spiritual scientists in intellectual affairs is so
difficult, on account of the dissipation of our
intellectual life.   Here we come to the painful
thought : How different these things would be
if scientists were really to become acquainted
with spiritual science, instead of passing it by
and leaving it to the foolish misrepresentations
of those who act in accordance with the axiom :
" Do not examine, but keep your irrelevant,
prejudiced verdict ! "   At the close of the
above-mentioned chapter Schleich says—and
the case is important, because there is no
question of ill-will, it is the statement of an
upright, true investigator—" If Goethe, that
seer and prophet, observed so many con-
nections in nature and demonstrated that the
skull with all its parts is nothing but an ex-
panded cervical vertebra, because all the
constituent parts of the latter can be traced in

the bony covering of the brain, it would not
surprise me if the thought I have just expressed, namely, of the heaping up of the
brain out of the elements of the spinal marrow,
did not also slip into the labyrinth of his
thought. I should not be surprised if some
day a slip of paper by Goethe on this subject
were found." Such is our intellectual co-
operation at the present time ! In 1916 an
honest searcher expects that some time a scrap
of paper of Goethe's will be found. But this
was found by me as long ago as 1891. In the
Goethian Annual for 1892, page 175, in the
article *Goethe as Anatomist*, written by Professor K. v. Bardeleben, you will read, " The
fact that Goethe occupied himself not only with
Osteology, but also with the ligaments, the
muscles, as well as the brain, is shown by
various notes, most of them on loose leaves.
In the *Venetian Diary* for 1790 R. Steiner
found the following sentence, which may be
closely connected with Goethe's thought on the
vertebral nature of the skull-bones : ' The
brain itself is only a large principal ganglion.
The organisation of the brain is repeated in
each ganglion, so that each ganglion is to be
looked upon as a small subordinate brain.' "
On the basis of this and similar things which
I found, I was able to write in 1897 in my
book, *Goethe's Conception of the World*, out of
purely scientific thought, " Each nerve-centre

in the ganglia was to him (Goethe) a brain at
a lower stage." And this, in addition to many
other things in connection with it, I have
often mentioned since. This is only intended
to be a small example of the manner in which
investigators talk in vain in our pursuit of
modern science. I shall certainly be the last
to reproach Schleich for not knowing *Goethe's
Annual* for 1892 and my book of 1897 ; the
uncertainty in our pursuit of science comes not
from people but from the conditions.

*   *   *

In this booklet it has been pointed out how
unfounded is all antagonism to spiritual
science proceeding from religious points of
view. We mentioned the excellent rectorial
address given in 1894 by a Catholic priest who
was professor to the theological faculty at
Vienna University. We are referring to
Doctor Laurenz Müllner and his discourse on
Galileo's Importance to Philosophy. In this
address Doctor Müllner, who has remained a
faithful son of his Church, says the following :
" Thus a new conception of the world appeared
(he is referring to the Galileo-Copernican
view), which in many points was apparently at
variance with opinions regarding which it
was asserted, with very questionable right,
that they proceeded from the doctrines of

Christianity. It was much more a question of the contrast of the widened world-consciousness of the *modern* age to the more limited one of the *antique*, a contrast to the Greek, but not to the rightly understood Christian conception of the world, which could only see fresh marvels of divine power and wisdom in the newly discovered starry worlds, whereby the miracle of divine love accomplished on earth could only acquire greater importance." In a similar manner with respect to the relation of spiritual science to religion it may be said that this spiritual science is often apparently at variance with opinions which are often represented as belonging to Christianity, but which with very questionable right assert their origin in the doctrines of Christianity. It is more a question of the contrast of the world-consciousness of our modern age which has extended into spiritual reality to the narrowly limited natural-scientific consciousness of the last few centuries, but not to the rightly understood Christian conception of the world, which should only see in the spirit-worlds of Anthroposophy new marvels of divine power and wisdom, whereby the miracle of divine love accomplished in the world of sense can only acquire enhanced importance. As soon as in certain directions there is a fundamental insight into spiritual science such as was possessed by the above-mentioned noble priest and theologian, Laurenz Müllner, into modern natural science, all the attacks which are often made in such an unfounded manner upon spiritual science from the standpoint of religion will cease.

The following mystical pictures are not related to this book.

They have been included for your enjoyment.

Pictures 1

Pictures 2

FAITH, HOPE, AND CHARITY.

Pictures 4

Pictures 5

ALCHYMIA
(From Thurneysser's Quinta Essentia, 1570)

Pictures 6

Pictures 7

Pictures 8

Pictures 9

Assyrian Type of Gilgamesh

Pictures 10

Pictures 11

MASONIC APRON PRESENTED TO GEN. WASHINGTON
BY MADAME LAFAYETTE.

Pictures 13

THE GOLDEN WHEEL

Pictures 15

Pictures 16

Pictures 17

Pictures 18

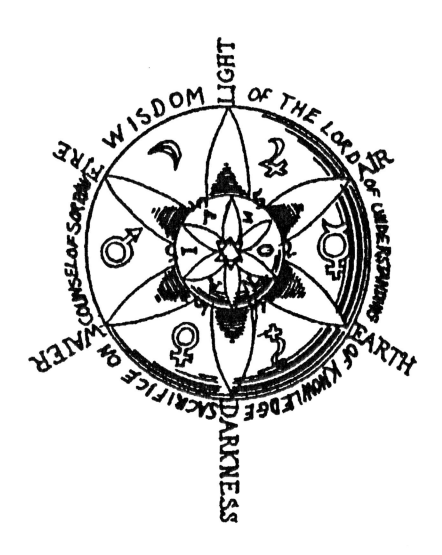

Pictures 19

Pictures 20

Pictures 21

Pictures 22

Pictures 23

Pictures 24

Pictures 25

MERCURIUS DE MERCURIO

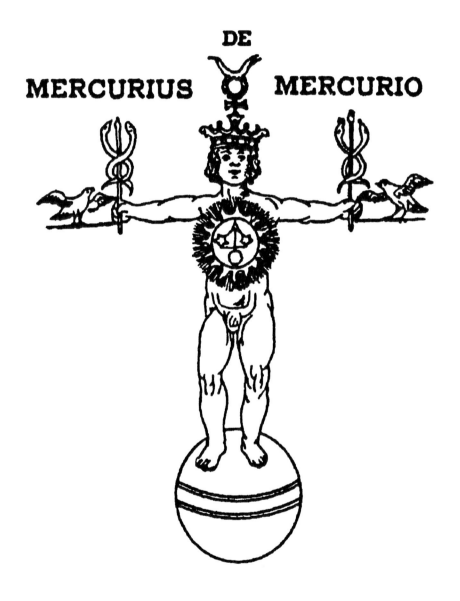

Pictures 26

Pictures 28

Pictures 29

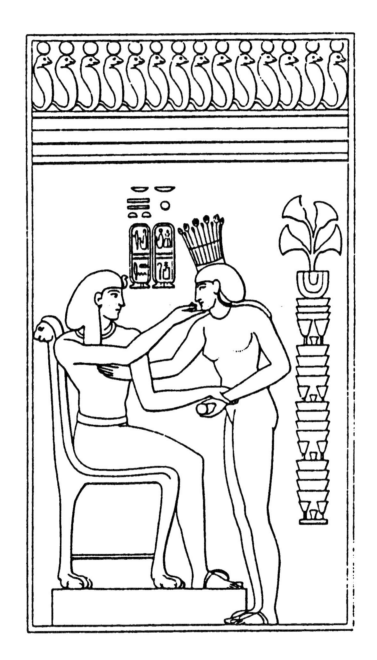

Pictures 30

Pictures 31

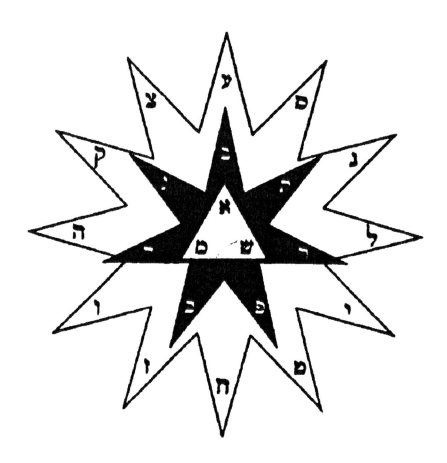

Pictures 32

Pictures 33

Pictures 34

Pictures 35

Pictures 36

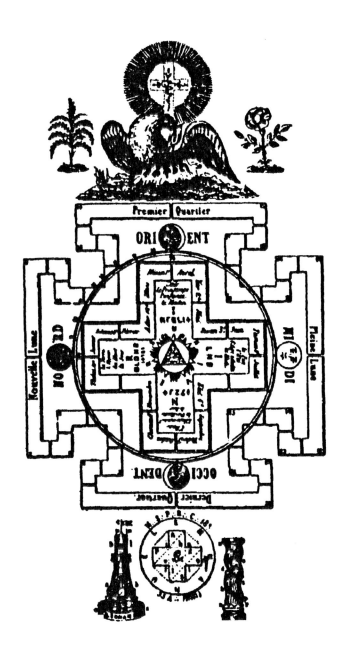

Pictures 37

Pictures 38

Pictures 39

Pictures 40

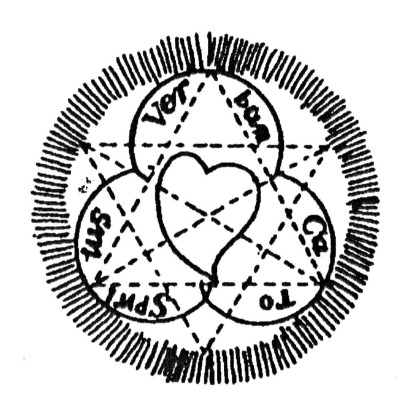

Pictures 41

Printed in the United Kingdom
by Lightning Source UK Ltd.
108572UKS00001B/11